POSITIONED for PURPOSE

The Journey

POSITIONED *for* PURPOSE

The Journey

A story of hope and triumph and finding purpose amidst life's difficulties.

COLETTE M. LAWRENCE

© Copyright 2021 by Colette Lawrence

All rights reserved.

It is not legal to reproduce, duplicate, or transmit any part of this document in either electronic means or printed format. Recording of this publication is strictly prohibited.

DEDICATION

Father, I give this book to you. You birthed something on the inside of me that you wanted me to share with the world. My, how you've shown me my heart and yours towards me all at the same time. Thank you for the words.

To my mother, Helen Samuels. Mom, when no one else would, you stood by me. You are still standing by me, and your fierce belief in me is only matched by my love for you. You never gave up on me, even when I gave you countless opportunities to. You have never shown or expressed disappointment in me, though I was sure you felt it. Your support will continue to be the wind beneath my wings. Thank you for being my covering through prayer, your words, and your love.

And to my two daughters, Nicola and Danielle. My rocks, vision pushers, stabilizers, and loyal supporters. Pushing when required and quietly encouraging when needed, it is truly appreciated. How you warm my heart with your dedication and love which is only matched by your desires to see me succeed. My love for you knows no

bounds. I love you fiercely my darlings, and I am so glad that He chose me for you.

FOREWORD

Colette provides a Spiritual and Visual journey that evokes joy, sadness, and victory, sometimes on one page. As Colette shares her discovery of who she was by discovering what she thought was her demise, the reader will begin to reflect on her own journey. The spiritual and emotional position of the reader will be revealed to her while reading this book and engaging in the end-of-chapter exercises.

No matter where the reader is right now in her Life's Journey "Positioned for Purpose" is a tool for a quantum leap in their current season.

Shirley Toliver

ACKNOWLEDGEMENT

Belinda Leyow, I couldn't have done this without you. Your patience, eye for detail, the copious questions you asked, and the countless hours you spent editing the first draft of this book is well appreciated. Thank you for sticking with me and for your desire to see me complete this. Words aren't enough to express my gratitude to you, all that I can say is that the Lord knew I needed you, and I am giving thanks that He placed you in my path.

Ekechi Pitt, what can I say about you and your desire to create a cover design that truly captures the story in this book. You are a young woman with exceptional creativity, and I want to thank you for depending on the Holy Spirit to bring the vision to life through your designs. Blessings on what I know will be a very bright future for you.

To all my family, friends, and prayer partners who encouraged, prayed for, read drafts, gave feedback, made introductions, and stood with me through this journey, thank you. Each of you has played a part in this journey, and the reality is that I couldn't have done it without the love and support of all of you. Blessings.

INTRODUCTION

Approximately 15 years ago, I started the process of documenting my journey. I had just gone through a divorce and felt the need to write. Unfortunately, the work was lost, and I didn't want to start all over to recapture my thoughts. Then came 2020, and the desire was renewed, and Positioned for Purpose moved from thought to words on paper.

This book isn't as I thought it would be. The focus was not on others and the hurt on pain, but more on me. Positioned for Purpose captured the journey from high school to now middle-aged years. It depicts a woman with emotional baggage and scars, lost identity, low self-confidence and worth, maybe like what you are going through or may have gone through. It is a reminder that none of our pain is discarded but will be used for God's greater glory if we will allow it to.

This book is about Romans 8:28 "For we know that all things work together for good to those that love God and are the called according to His purpose. The message I hope it conveys is that no matter what our past or even our current lives look like, there is a purpose behind the pain. Looking back, things were difficult, and I felt so many times like giving up, and dare I say that sometimes I just didn't care anymore. The hurt can sometimes allow us to feel as if God has abandoned us, which is not the case, but that is what the devil wants us to think.

What I hope that you take away from this book is that there is hope. Your current circumstances or situations are no match for God's love for you and the plan that He has for your life. Each hurt, mistake, broken heart, bruised ego, each loss that you suffered is working out for your greater good. I know that you might not see it now, or maybe you have. It was hard for me to believe that good could come out of the bad situations that I got myself in or suffered from. It took me much later to realize that no matter what, there was a good plan set for me, my view was blocked and limited by my past, my rearview mirror was darkened, however, when I decided to look forward on the road ahead, I realized that life was not as dismal and hopeless as I thought. Yes, God has a good plan in store, not just for me but for you as well.

Let us agree not to keep looking back in the rearview mirror so that we will not miss what lies ahead of us. There are seasons in our lives, the skies won't always be blue, and neither will there always be sunshine. There is one thing that we know when we look up and see a rainbow, we are reminded of a promise made long ago. So today, the promise to us is that pain has paved the way and has positioned you not only to walk in but also to live out your purpose. So, go ahead and do that, impact the lives of your daughters, your sisters, your mother, your girlfriends and whoever else God has called you to serve. Come on, we are waiting on you. Position your yourself for the purpose that you were created for and the impact that you will make in your generation.

CONTENTS

Dedication i
Foreword iii
Acknowledgement v
Introduction vii

CHAPTER 1: ALABASTER BOX 1

    The Journey 2
    The Catalyst 4
    Losing Me 5
    Lessons Learned 9

CHAPTER 2: LOST AND FOUND 11

    Comparison 11
    Reflections of Me 14
    Identity Restored 15
    Lessons Learned 17

CHAPTER 3: BREAKING FREE 19

    Decluttering 19
    Restoring Me 21
    Lessons Learned 24

CHAPTER 4: THE DARK PLACE 25

    The Pain 25
    The Story 26

Lessons Learned..31

CHAPTER 5: LOVE IN A BOX 33
The Flutters...33
The Warm and Fuzzy 35
My Plans..36
The Decision 38
Lessons Learned..42

CHAPTER 6: NO CONDEMNATION 45
The Weight 45
Moving On 47
The Love of God 48
Lessons Learned..51

CHAPTER 7: THE SEASONS OF OUR LIVES 53
Ebb and Flow 53
The Questions..54
Drawn Closer to My Father and Friend 55
Thanksgiving 57
Lessons Learned..59

CHAPTER 8: POSITIONED FOR PURPOSE....................61
The Word 61
The Path 62
Positioned 63
Walking in Purpose..64
Lessons Learned..65

Conclusion 67

My Prayer For Us...71

CHAPTER 1

Alabaster Box

Listening to Cece Winans belting out those heartfelt lyrics to her song, "Alabaster Box," I felt she was singing about me. Tears rolled down my face as I remembered the downward trajectory I was on. Years later, this song still resonates deeply because it speaks of the grace of the Lord who found me. Truth be told, I should not be standing.

My life was a mess, and I felt like giving up many times. Frankly, I do not know what anyone saw in me then. I saw myself as nothing and as nobody. I was involved with the wrong people, in wrong relationships, making wrong choices, and with seemingly no care in the world about what my future would look like if I did not get off the current path I was on. Young and naïve, I was a college dropout and a teenage mom. Wow, that sounds like a lot. Anyway, it is what it is. Up to that time, my claim to fame was that I smoked a cigarette once, had my first drink, and of course, I got drunk. Ooh, the story on that one, but after that, the strongest drink was Apple Cider (smile).

Growing up in Jamaica, I searched for acceptance and love in all the wrong places and things. Looking back, it is amazing that I am still alive. Whatever purpose we were created for, we all have an opportunity to accomplish it. Can I be real with you? I used to wonder why the Lord loves me so much. I seemed to be making all the wrong choices and couldn't understand why He continued to give me grace (I needed) each day. I felt truly unworthy of His grace and His mercy.

It's a good thing that the Lord gives second chances; He knew I needed a whole lot of those, sigh. The statement, 'purpose can't die' is very real to me because it reminds me that I am here for a reason: so are you.

THE JOURNEY

Let's get started. I can only remember bits and pieces of my childhood. I wasn't living with my mother full time, but there was one thing I knew for sure; my mother loved me. The summers that I spent with her were the best times of my life, and she was affectionate and caring. I was raised by relatives who demonstrated their love by providing food, shelter, and clothing. They treated me the same way they were raised; they didn't know differently. Looking back, I now realize that affection meant more to me than the physical provisions they gave.

My morning routine was the same every day. The schedule was set; make the bed, and clean the living room, which was called a hall in those days, followed by cleaning the verandah, aka the porch. It concluded with having breakfast, showering, and getting my hair combed. That part was my least favorite, rake, rake, rake with the comb. My aunt would say, "Stand still, hold your head straight." Oh my, how I dreaded those mornings, but my hair had to be combed, no two ways about it.

It was a pleasure going to school though, walking with my friends in the morning and making the over 10-mile journey, five days each week. When you have someone walking with you, the journey feels shorter, less burdensome. Walking alone, it seems to take longer to get to your destination. John Doone's song, "No Man Is an Island, No Man Stands Alone," reminds us that we need each other in this race called life.

Each summer was spent with my mom in Kingston, Jamaica. It was the highlight of my year. To be in her calming presence, and to also spend time with my brother was something that I looked forward to. I cherished the memories of those visits because the time was always enjoyable. Although I can't recall specific activities, to this day, it brings a smile to my lips as I reminisce. There were things that I was sure of (1) I

Colette M. Lawrence

looked forward to going, (2) I loved being with my mom, and (3) I did not want to return. When summer ended and I had to go home, it was bittersweet and the hardest thing to bear. I remember feeling a bit of excitement on returning to the country. It felt like I had traveled overseas, and I could not wait to boast about the trip to my friends.

THE CATALYST

Little did I know it, but the summer of 1980 was going to change things. A young man who had the *nerve* to write me a love letter came on the scene. Oh my, he couldn't have known that the letter would change my life for the better. The things and people that the Lord can use to change the trajectory of our lives never ceases to amaze me. I put the letter away in the top right-hand corner of the dresser in my room. I still don't know how my aunt found it, but she did. She said, "You're not going to stay here and get pregnant, you are going to live with your mother!" That made my day. The letter should never have been written because its contents were above my age level. Nevertheless, the discovery of this letter resulted in an unintended yet much-desired outcome; I got to live with my mom.

The plans were put in motion, and my cousin was coming to take me home. As much as I dreaded the letter being discussed, the thought of being with my mom far outweighed that. I sat at the back of that baby blue bus, watching the scenery and anticipating the reunion. The ride took forever and a day, but it did not matter. Every moment was worth the wait. To say that I was happy was an understatement. Who cared about a love letter? All I knew was that the desires of my heart were being granted, and that was perfectly fine with me. It was an opportunity to start over, although at that age, I certainly did not know what that meant. A new environment, new home, new family members, and new school were awaiting me. Adjusting at school was difficult, and in my first year, I struggled to form relationships. After the initial struggle, I settled into a routine and made friends. Life was good. It was great being a kid, carefree, loved, and provided for.

New environments require change, a new mindset, relinquishing the past, the weights, and the setbacks. As I grew older and made the transition from Kingston to St. Catherine, Jamaica, it would be another adjustment period. This one would prove to be more difficult than the previous one. There would be a new community, a new school, and the process of finding new friends all over again. The first two years of high school were rough. I was teased relentlessly by girls and boys who called me all kinds of names based on how I looked. I had serious acne. Kids can be truly unkind and hurtful, which is why it is so important to tell our children to treat someone else the same way they want to be treated. No one understood how I felt. They assumed it was a phase and would pass, but it did not. I internalized those comments and believed that I was ugly. I found comfort however, in reading novels until the wee hours of the morning. It was the escape route, and I ran to it every evening after school.

LOSING ME

Losing value in yourself puts you in a position to make decisions that will either damage you, scar you for life, kill you mentally, emotionally, and even physically. I started searching for someone who would see me as beautiful. My self-image was deteriorating, and I needed someone, *anyone*, to affirm that I was beautiful. As a teenager, I wanted validation, and it didn't matter how much my mom loved me or that she thought I was beautiful. In my head, she is family and is expected to say that. The desire was to hear it from someone else. Little did I know that at my age, hearing that would come at a price, and it would cost me something.

Thankfully, I finished high school, then moved to live with my grandparents to attend a nearby college. Adjusting to college life was hard and was proving to be a challenge. I finally started assimilating, but my time in college would be short-lived, and I would soon face a much bigger challenge.

At 18, just one month before my 19th birthday, I became a teenage mom. I remember that day clearly, hearing the news that I was pregnant. Sitting in the doctor's office, all I could think about was what I was going to say to my parents and grandparents. That was the last news I expected or wanted to hear, but somehow should have anticipated it. This was devasting for me as I knew it would be for them. I was only one month into the first semester of college. Everyone, including myself, had high hopes for me; now, their hope and mine were dashed. I travelled back to the college to collect my things, and those few classmates that were around wanted to know what was wrong. Not quite six weeks into the first semester, I felt embarrassed to say that I was pregnant.

Bags packed, I walked out of the dorm room and walked into the unknown, with no clue of what was ahead of me. I now had this life growing inside me that I was totally responsible for. A teen mom, college dropout, and a young girl who did not know who she was, it seemed like the cards were stacked against me. In those days, if you were to gamble on me amounting to anything worthwhile in society, you would have safely placed your bet against me. My life was in a downward spiral, and here I was bringing a child into the world, with no idea what life would mean and look like for him or her.

Stares that seemed to burn deep within my soul, taunts, and whispers, coupled with nausea and fatigue were at times too much to bear, but what was I to do? The reality is, if you play with fire, you will get burned, and I had to live with the consequences of my actions. The months seemed to roll slowly by leaving too much time for my thoughts and the what if's. Then June 30th rolled around. She was here, and I loved her the moment I laid eyes on her, totally forgetting that I was just a child myself.

Life changed for me the day she came into the world, and just reflecting on the journey with my daughter brings tears to my eyes and a glimmer of a smile to my lips. She was a happy baby, quiet and content. There was and still is a fierce instinct to protect her, and now that I have two daughters, to protect them both. Wherever we went, people fell in love with her. She was well behaved and an absolute delight.

Motherhood forcefully plunged me into adulthood, I was now a woman in a child's body. Now, I had responsibilities too big for my age, however, as I grew as a mom, parenting matured me. It also brought along a steadiness I hadn't realized I needed because it forced me to make decisions. I still didn't know my worth, and it would take years to get me to that place, but a subtle change had already begun. I had grown. Motherhood can do that if we allow it to.

The journey wasn't easy. Many mistakes, poor decisions, and wrong choices were made. I hurt a lot of people, and a lot of people hurt me. One thing I learned much later is to not dwell in regret. Regret can't change the past, but you can use what you have learned from your past to change the present and your future.

Mark 14:3 speaks of the woman with an alabaster box of ointment who broke that box and used that precious oil to pour on Jesus' head. Reflecting on this portion of my life, the heartache, hardships, rejection, and my choices, I know that without God's help, I would not have made it. I would be the woman that would not be allowed into the room. However, His grace has granted me access to pour out my treasure of alabaster on Him, i.e., my praise. My praise will always be unapologetically loud because I have so much to thank God for. The truth is, I shouldn't be alive to share my journey with you, but there is a greater purpose for me. There is also a greater purpose for you too. This purpose is what the Lord wants us to use to draw others to Him.

Colette M. Lawrence

LESSONS LEARNED

Learn to love, accept and value yourself. Everything else will fall into place. Surround yourself with people who will add value to your life.

If you are a teenage mom, don't let that deter you from your dreams. If you have support, return to college. Fulfill your dreams while raising and loving your child fiercely. Trust me, after the storm, you will have a testimony.

Let no one define you by your past but USE your past as a stepping-stone to your future. I am not telling you that it will be easy, but I can tell you that it will be worth it.

CHAPTER 2
Lost And Found

Timid, shy, doubtful, and fearful are words that are used to describe me. I had low self-esteem, and somewhere along the way, I lost my voice. You may ask, how does losing my voice correlate with all those adjectives? Lean in close, let me whisper to you, I lost my voice when I lost me.

COMPARISON

We live in an era where physical beauty is idolized. Everywhere we go, we are bombarded with the promotion of and demand for physical beauty. You must have a flawless complexion. There is a television advertisement with every flick of the channel in our faces telling us what we need to do to obtain unblemished outward beauty. As a young woman, I began measuring myself against other young women. I thought having a flawless complexion was all there was to life; being beautiful became of the utmost importance. I fought hard to attain the perfect look, but it always eluded me. In school, I was teased about my looks. To this day, I cringe at the things said, for instance, "your face is ugly like a frog's back," and a name I later wore like a cloak, "crocodile face." Those words haunted me for years. They eroded my self-esteem, and eventually, I lost sight of who I was.

Of course, once you start comparing yourself to someone else, you are now measuring yourself using another person's standards. The background and issues of the person I was comparing myself to meant nothing to me. I slowly allowed myself to be drawn into a sea of self-pity. Soon, 'Ms. Less Than' joined me there followed by 'Ms. Not Good Enough', and finally, 'Ms. Ugly' came along too. Having acne back then was considered one of the seven deadly sins. It was akin to having the plague or some other very serious disease that no one wanted to catch. I was always confident and self-assured when I changed schools, but this was prior to hearing, "you have bumps." At first, these words did not mean anything to me until I understood that having acne meant that I was no longer beautiful. Imagine a teenager dealing with this and struggling to find footing in a new environment, and you have a recipe for self-hate.

All the self-confidence and assuredness that I had, was suddenly peeled away, layer by layer. No one knew the struggles I was facing. In fact, to listen to me talk then, you would have thought that I had it all together, but that was in the daytime. When night fell, all my fears came tumbling out. Of course, my parents affirmed me, but it had no impact because I wanted the acceptance of my peers. The question in my mind was, why can't they accept me? I just didn't see how my close friends looked beyond my un-attractiveness. Really, what *did* they see in me? Yes, their affirmations comforted and reassured, but only in the moment. What value did that have? Not much, because I wanted everyone's acceptance, and this need dominated for much of my life.

Negative words spoken over our lives have negative consequences, especially when you are already in a low place and cannot lift yourself from where you are. Couple that with the need for general acceptance, and I was now in an even darker place.

One Sunday in church, when I was about 20 years old, I remember standing for prayer. I was asked what I was believing God for. It was so embarrassing to say that I was praying for money to go to the dermatologist. At the time, it felt like all eyes were on me, my soul laid bare for everyone to see. It was as if I could hear them screaming, "What! So many things to pray for, and you are worried about your appearance."

I know, I know, I was judging them, right? Yes, I agree, I was allowing my imagination to run away with me.

I went back to my seat, dejected. I had no money, no doctor, and no solution. It was one more day of looking at my face. At the time, it seemed as if all people saw was my face. They didn't really see me. In conversation with them, I imagined them asking, "can't she do something about her face?" Can I tell you that those were some of the toughest years of my life? It became obvious that how I looked was adversely affecting me, and I had to find a way to deal with my struggles.

REFLECTIONS OF ME

Negative self-talk and low self-esteem followed me straight into adulthood. While I felt somewhat confident in myself, it never really felt like I fit in. I didn't believe that I belonged in the room, even though I had a seat at the table. I had already lost my identity, and now, I was slowly starting to lose my voice. Now that I am older and wiser, I wonder why I allowed what others thought about me to have so much influence over my life. Why didn't I choose to see the best in me and not permit my outward appearance or other people's opinions to define who I am? How in God's name did I allow this to happen? I do not have the answer.

"Thank you for making me so wonderfully complex! Your workmanship is marvelous, how well I know it" (Psalm 139:14 NLT). This is a scripture that I looked to for comfort. In the adult Sunday school class, the teacher read this passage, and since then, that verse has held a special place in my heart. It reminded me that while my concern was about my external beauty, I *was* created beautiful. Believing otherwise and calling myself anything less was essentially declaring that the Word of God is not true. It took a very long time for me to grab hold of that truth because my warped self-belief became so ingrained in who I was, that we couldn't be separated.

I had forgotten who I was and lost me. I made bad decisions and continued making bad decisions because I didn't value myself. There came a time when I had to let go of my past and examine the lessons I was being taught because that negativity helped shape me and how I viewed myself.

IDENTITY RESTORED

Going through this pandemic in 2020 has been a deciding season in my life. I did not want to enter a new season the same way I had done before. One morning, I was reading a LinkedIn post. The author wrote about losing his voice, and he shared the reason he lost it. That article exposed my hurt and revealed to me that I had also lost my voice. Prayerfully, I asked the Lord to tell me how and at what point I lost the ability to be who he created me to be. The answer came as I stepped in the shower that morning; I lost my voice when I believed I was a nobody. I lost myself and believed the lies the enemy fed me. This revelation touched a chord deep in my soul.

The weight of this hit me hard. I didn't lose my voice because my parents thought less of me, nor did I lose sight of myself because kids were unkind to me. I lost both when I allowed others to define me with their opinion of what beauty looks like. I internalized all those feelings until they became *my* thoughts, and ultimately, I became my thoughts. Proverbs 23:7 says, "As he thinks in his heart, so is he" (NKJV). As I showered, armed with this newfound knowledge, my morning seemed to pause as I went back in time. Every lather laid bare the past, and with every rinse, that past was stripped and washed away. I stepped out of the shower with a renewed confidence in who I am, and an awakened voice to speak responsibly *and* boldly. I got dressed, my identity buttoned in place, and my voice back to normal.

I found my voice that day and chose to use it wisely. I will be careful of the things I say, because my words have life and power, and they have impact. They can either tear you down or build you up, and I choose to use them to build you up. My words can either be used to water the soil or cause drought, I will use them to water soil. My choice is to use this voice as a life-giving source.

I remember asking the Lord, what do you want me to do in this season, and His response was, "Use your voice." So today, I choose to use my voice to say to you, don't allow anyone to define who you are or your value. You were uniquely created, and you are fearfully and wonderfully made, a true masterpiece.

- You deserve a place in the room.
- You deserve a seat at the table.
- You are confident and self-assured.
- You are an overcomer and a winner.
- Your inner beauty radiates like a beacon of light drawing others in.
- You are the light that the world is waiting on, so shine forth.

I see you; I hope that you see yourself. I hear you; I hope that you hear yourself. Come, let's change the world together with our collective and united voices.

Colette M. Lawrence

LESSONS LEARNED

Always affirm yourself, and don't wait on someone else to do it. Outward appearance carries significant weight in society, and we can get drawn into this. As parents, we believe our children should rise above what society dictates, but they are not always able to do so. I learned to instill those values in my own children, yet have seen that even when parents do this, some will still be guided by the world's view.

Our identity is like our DNA, revealing who we each uniquely are. If that image becomes marred or scarred in any way, it creates problems that we sometimes pay dearly for. Let us raise our children, particularly our girls, to value themselves and see themselves as beautiful creations made by our heavenly Father. We are indeed created in His own image and likeness. Thus, we are fearfully and wonderfully made (Psalm 139:14 KJV).

CHAPTER 3

Breaking Free

It was 2:00 A.M. and thoughts were swirling in my mind, like voices screaming, "What if, what if!" No rest, no peace. How could I arrest this cacophony of sounds in my mind? It seemed those thoughts were all jostling for attention, for first place, top priority. What was I to do with these deafening sounds? You must be wondering, is she crazy or possessed? You might say this is nonsense, but for me, it wasn't.

DECLUTTERING

Does your mind take you back to a close relative who experienced this? Was she declared mentally unfit? Could it be you also struggled or are still struggling with voices that want to get loose? But I am not that 'close relative,' just plain scared to acknowledge thoughts which are a culmination of all my fears, insecurities, and episodes of rejection. I had silenced them for so long that they were now screaming for my attention. How on earth can I face these thoughts when I don't know how to handle them? I knew they must be stopped, but I was too afraid to let them out of the cocoon that I called my mind.

It's was 4:00A.M., and I couldn't stand it anymore. I placed my hand over my ears as if to drown out the noise, but that was not enough to dull the pain and quiet the sounds raging to get out. Pain...what pain? Pain just sounds like a figment of my imagination. If it bothered me so much, why didn't I simply deal with it? And if it was so loud and distressing, why did I allow it to torture me so? It's not as easy as you think. I wanted to stop the noise, but you see, stopping the noise might have just stopped my heart.

The fear of taking it from the box and exposing it would mean I now had to face what I was running and hiding from. The question then became, what has me bound and has such control over me? The answer is FEAR, or False Evidence Appearing Real. My life had been dominated by this monster for a long time. I allowed it to run roughshod over me, afraid of taking a step because all I could think of were worst case scenarios. I thought of failure; I would never make it, they won't respect me, they will laugh, no one will listen, nobody will see me.

There comes a time when you become sick and tired of being sick and tired. That time was now, time to break free from the prison of my own mind. But wait, how do I break out and unpack years of this inner turmoil; where and how do I start? The decision was made, but I was afraid to take the first step. I got up one morning and knew that was the day change was going to take place. It was now or never. I slowly began exposing every demon of fear: "I am a failure, I am not good enough, they won't like me, I'm too ugly, they will reject me, they don't want me in the room, no one wants me." As these thoughts surfaced, I realized that they were False Evidence Appearing Real. I asked the Holy Spirit to help me because those tormenting noises in my head had to go. Verbalizing those thoughts loudly and hearing all the negativity and limiting self-beliefs I held about myself, made me realize I was tightly bound. I had to be released. I called on the Lord to come near and help me from these grave clothes of emotions. And come He did. He called me out of the tomb of self-loathing to a renewed life of acceptance and self-love.

RESTORING ME

Once you embark on the journey of decluttering your mind, you must see it through to the end, or it will create future obstacles. The negative thinking had to be replaced with words of affirmation. The key was not only in identifying the lies but going a step further, replacing those lies with the truth of who I am. So, for every lie, there must be a truth to replace it.

LIE	TRUTH
I am not good enough.	I am more than enough.
I am ugly.	I am beautiful inside and out.
No one hears.	Yes, someone hears me.
No one sees.	Yes, someone sees me.
I am nothing.	I am someone, and I am

John 10:10b states, "I have come that they may have life, and that they may have *it* more abundantly" (NKJV). When death-inducing words are thrown out, then life-giving words inhabit those dead spaces, flooding them with the light of God's truth. From here on, attitudes must change. In the beginning, our brains are like children learning to take their first step, who will one day walk, then run. Those first steps will be worth it in the end. Every day I fought by pushing past the lies, choosing to speak affirming words over myself, and believing them like my life depended on it. It takes time to change a narrative which took years to build up, so I won't tell you or even suggest that it will be easy. I *can* tell you, it will be bear fruit. Let's now take time to

know who we were created to be and become secure in that knowledge.

There is something that happens when written words are spoken. When we give voice to thoughts that are clear and positive, they possess depth and power to liberate and transform you feel reborn. The Bible says, "Death and life are in the power of the tongue, and those who love it will eat its fruit" (Proverbs 18:21 NKJV). I went through the process of not only writing but speaking the following over my life, and can attest that it made a real difference. So today, declare with me, "I am fearfully and wonderfully made. I am the apple of God's eye. I am the righteousness of God in Christ Jesus. Whether they see me or not, I am here, and I am present. Whether they hear me or not, I have a voice, and I will use it. I am more than enough. I am capable. I have greatness lying on the inside of me. I will make it."

The choice is ours to determine if we will allow fear to grab hold of us and take us captive as prisoners in our own minds. I chose to chase out the defeating chatter, replacing it with life-giving thoughts allowed to roam freely. Fear, doubts, and self-limiting beliefs no longer have a hold on me. I broke free, and so can you.

Colette M. Lawrence

LESSONS LEARNED

If permitted, fear and doubt will run us into the ground. I had allowed these spirits to torment me and hold me captive for so long, in places that I should have broken free from. Fear, low self-esteem, and lack of confidence were things that dominated my life during this period. 2 Timothy 1:7 states, "God has not given us a spirit of fear, but of power and of love and of a sound mind" (NKJV). Even though I was unsure if I understood what it really meant, I repeated this scripture to myself continually. Isaiah 55:11 assures, "So shall my word be that goes forth from my mouth, it shall not return to Me void, but it shall accomplish what I please" (NKJV).

The Word, along with having accountability partners, were the tools I used through the years to help me overcome. It works, but it takes time.

Trust the process and replace negative thinking with the positive Word of God.

Believe what the word of God says about who we are.

CHAPTER 4

The Dark Place

I remember it like it was only yesterday. Each day when the girls left for school, I found myself under the dining room table, hiding. Lost in a dark place, my world was crumbling, and I wanted to die. My mind swirled with suicidal thoughts, at which point life held no real meaning for me. Living hurt, and I didn't want to continue. My heart ached, my head was pounding, and I had what felt like a million thoughts competing to be heard and intent on driving me crazy.

THE PAIN

It took everything in me to get up, feed the kids and send them off to school. I felt lost for the remainder of the day. Was it possible to feel simultaneously sane and insane? Days ran into each other, and I was holding on by a thread. That dining room table seemed to provide some level of protection, a sort of refuge from life, an escape from the world. It didn't, however, offer any relief from the emotional turmoil or noise in my head. Depressed and heartbroken, I was a woman overrun by loss. I felt alone in the world.

Did anyone know what was happening with me or notice how much quieter and withdrawn I had become? Did they see the pain in my eyes and hear the hurt in my voice? If they saw, did they really care? Who could I unburden myself to, who would understand? This burden was not something easily shared or discussed. I didn't have the energy anyway to provide answers to spoken or unspoken questions. Depression was a dark place, a tunnel. It lured, and I ran to it; it was a place to hide from my challenges.

The breakup of a marriage is devastatingly hard. It is not something I wish on anyone. The emotional, spiritual, psychological, and even physical toll it can take on the entire being is almost more than one can bear, especially when children are also involved. People don't plan for failed relationships, yet they happen, and each of us has our own experiences at different stages in life.

THE STORY

August 5, 1995, was one of the happiest days of my life. Surprisingly, even twenty-six years later, the events of that day are still fresh in my mind. I looked forward to that day with every fiber of my being. I was in love, happy, content. The future looked bright. I had found my happily ever after, and I was looking forward to spending my life with him. The song in my head at the time may have been Crystal Gayle's, "A Long and Lasting Love." Smiles.

It was a clear sunny afternoon, perfect for a small wedding attended by close family and friends. The ceremony was beautiful and the reception enjoyable. Looking back, everything wasn't ideal, but it worked well for us. All the people who were important in our lives were there to witness our union. We were excited about our future together as we went on a honeymoon at a dear friend's home, which was their wedding gift to us.

Marriage was good, and we settled into a routine of family, church, work, and home. We adjusted to each other well, and I daresay that we were happy. I already had my first child and planned to start adding to the family later, but it did not work out that way because within a year, we had our first child together, my second daughter. We were now a family of four, and our marriage seemed to be steadying well, but over time, the road became rocky. Tensions flew, and life got difficult. Early on, we made a commitment that no matter what happened between us, divorce would never be an option. It simply wouldn't be. Counseling helped, however, underlying issues once shrouded, were now wreaking havoc and destroying our lives. In hindsight,

Colette M. Lawrence

I missed all the signs that were in clear view. Sometimes, we only see what we want to see, and sometimes, we don't believe that what we see is real. Life throws us curve balls and lemons too. Often, they arrive at the same time, but *we choose* how we will respond. It's a matter of survival, whether we sink or swim, and o*nly we* can determine the outcome. If you asked at that moment what my choice would be, I would give the obvious answer, with my hands on my hips and a vehement shake of my head, "SWIM, I choose to swim!"

2001 would prove to be a year I had to fight to hold on for my dear life. It felt like a freight train hit me from behind *and* head on. Either way, I didn't see it coming and I couldn't run out of the way, *SPLAT!* Once that train stopped, I needed the Lord's hand to gently check that all my parts were still intact. Bruised, battered and near dead inside, only He had resurrection power to breathe life back into me.

There I was, under the table with tears streaming down my face, wishing life would just pass me by. For days, I didn't shower but lay in bed, wanting neither visitors nor calls, desiring only to be left alone to wallow in misery. My best friend and three other close friends came to visit, and I wondered how they endured the stench of my unwashed body in that dark room. They prayed for me then left; strength gently surged through my body. That night, my life changed. Their prayer heralded hope and signaled the dawning of a new day. The next morning, I slowly got out of bed, showered, then changed the bed linens, and that night, I slept well. Despite this, the next day brought a harsh reminder that the hurt had not been erased, and I would need to determine what my next steps were.

Change had taken place, and our family of four had now become a family of three. Life would not be easy. In fact, it was an uphill battle, a battle that would require every ounce of strength as well as a support team to move on and rebuild. In those days, my daughters were my everything; they still are. As I slowly started to rebuild my life, I knew that I had to be better, not just for them but also for me. There were days I lapsed, but I'm grateful that the Lord Jesus held onto my hand. Depression is no walk in the park. It's a dark place where you can easily lose yourself and your identity, while it robs you of your joy and your peace. The way out requires assistance along the way because one slip could take you down a path that I don't wish on anyone. Every day called for intentionality. I determined to put one foot in front of the other and, I also chose to allow others in, to help carry me through.

There were people who counselled, encouraged, and prayed with me daily. They stayed until I was able to 'walk' again. Despite my stubbornness, arguments, and the doubts I shared, I am grateful they didn't leave me when the dark place beckoned once more. With my Lord and Savior Jesus undergirding me and with the support of family and friends, I landed on my own two feet. This support system ensured that I would not succumb to the darkness at the end of what appeared an endless tunnel. There was a bright light shining, one of hope, peace, and a reminder of God's presence. It continues to lead and light the path before me.

I needed that light for when the divorce would ultimately come. If you have ever been depressed and you know without a shadow of a doubt that it was only by the grace and mercy of the Lord Jesus Christ that you made it, be thankful. If you are going through depression, do not give up; hold on, you are NOT alone. The Lord God whom I serve is rich to all who call on Him, He will never leave you or forsake you, and He will never let you go. Surround yourself with people who love you and want the best for you. Take it one day at a time and one step at a time. While the reasons we go through depression are wide and vary, so are also the emotions we experience, you *can* make it out. It could be difficult, and you may not be able to do it on your own. Build a support team and lean on the Lord Jesus Christ.

The divorce took a hard toll, replacing peace and joy with heartache and loneliness. It caused me to again question my value; was I enough? It affected us as a family, but I thank God that He kept our unit of three together. We weathered the storm and are still standing firm because the God of all hope preserved us. Our purpose was not aborted, we live to laugh again, to smile again, and to love again.

POSITIONED For PURPOSE

Colette M. Lawrence

LESSONS LEARNED

Seek the Lord for a mate; just because a person is a Christian doesn't automatically mean you are destined to be together.

Patiently wait on God's timing and His perfect will.

Surround yourself with a support system. This period of my life taught me that I can't live my life alone. Your support system can make the difference in whether you stand or fall, sink or swim.

Divorce does not define who we are, and it does not dictate our future.

CHAPTER 5

Love In A Box

I wonder how I fell into the relationships I did, fast and deep, then crash landing. It seemed to be the story of my life. Each time was supposed to be different, and one time, I thought it was, but that's another story for another day. Love finds a way into our hearts. There is a song, "Love Has Finally Come at Last," about the arrival of love and the determination to hold on to it. I always looked for that type of love, the long and lasting kind. You know, the one they say few find. Well, I thought I found it, only to miss again! There are days when I question if I will ever find covenant love that truly epitomizes God's plan for me.

THE FLUTTERS

To love and be loved is a beautiful thing, don't you agree? In the right context and with the right person, you believe there is no obstacle you can't overcome, no barrier that can't be broken down, and no devil you can't defeat. There is nothing like the feeling of belonging. Our hearts are always searching for the one we can make life and music with, the one that is bringing their 100% authentic self. Some people find that person the first time around and know without a shadow of a doubt they belong together. They find what we call the "until death mentality." Others are still seeking, and still, some of us thought we found it, only to be scorned by it.

There are days I ask myself if I will ever have that type of love, the kind my grandparents and parents have. It has been one of the many prayers that I prayed, uhm I'm still praying. Smile. Let's face it, we are built for relationships, and there are days when I would like to lean over with a tender look into my eyes, and a sweet smile on my lips and whisper, I love you my dear. Ahh, if only.

Sometimes I feel the Lord is holding out on me, but maybe I didn't wait the first time around. Instead, I made my choice and reaped the results. Perhaps there are areas in me and the other person He needs to work on, so that when we meet, we will fit: two wholes becoming one. Yes, we need to see the glass as half full and look at the positives. I know, I know, I hear you, just be patient and wait. Surely the Lord knows my heart's desire. He also knows how I ponder about the *who* and the *when*.

Have you ever felt that you have everything, family, friends, community, yet you still feel alone? I have. It feels like something is missing. I know we must be content in whatever state we are in; however, that does not mean that we can't talk about our situation while we pray and wait. After making so many bad choices, I am learning what it means to truly wait on God and his timing and to trust his promises for my life. Waiting is not always easy but let's discuss the other side of the coin. Let's discuss walking out of His will for our lives. Have you ever done this? Oftentimes it ends in ways that hurt us, and we pay the penalty. Do you agree? Truth be told, I paid the price for wanting and taking what was not meant for me. I had walked out on God's will for me before because my heart wanted what it wanted, without the thought of consequences. The enemy of our souls loves when we get emotionally tied because then we fall out of relationship with God and *gotcha*! he has us, hook, line, and sinker.

THE WARM AND FUZZY

He was a friend I cared for deeply. The first time I saw him, I knew he was special. I remember precisely what he looked like, and what he wore; it still brings a smile to my lips. We could talk for hours. Well, maybe that was mostly me because I am a talker. *Anyway,* we could talk about anything. Not one dimensional, he was a deep thinker who pushed the envelope in our conversations. I was challenged to be more objective and broaden my outlook to see the bigger picture. You could tell from his conversation that he was an avid reader. Always a pleasure to be around, and I was glad to call him a friend. There was a level of trust between us and a bond of friendship I believe we both enjoyed.

As time went by, I realized I wanted more than just friendship, and I hoped the feeling was mutual. They say hindsight is 20/20. In retrospect, I must admit that *I* pursued him. Ouch! I wanted a future with him, but he did not want that. Had I been paying attention and not so caught up in myself, I would have recognized he did not feel the same. It would be great to be able to say he loved me the way I loved him, but that would not be true. He loved me only as a friend. That realization was painful, and I asked myself repeatedly, "How did I get here?" The question was not hard to ask, it was accepting the answer that was difficult. When we are in a low place, and someone gives us attention, sometimes we take it to mean more than it should. We make mistakes, cross boundary lines, and then fall into traps that could take years to unravel.

The need to be loved and be part of a unit was something that I longed for. The attention was exhilarating; I allowed it to go to my head. Drunk with the thoughts and feelings of young love (smile), I was going full speed ahead into a head-on collision. Have you been there? Ever had the desire and need to feel that sense of belonging and security that a right relationship gives? It's tough, isn't it? I allowed my desire to become a need which overrode what I knew to be true. Anything other than God that we place too much emphasis on, and have too much desire for, becomes an idol in our lives.

MY PLANS

As time passed, I found myself planning our future, all in my mind, of course. There *was* no proposal, but apparently, that was lost on me. I really don't know why I thought he would change his mind. I find that as women, sometimes we hang on to relationships and things beyond their expiration date because we believe we will be the ones to bring change.

Sometimes we hear what we want to hear, and I know that can come from a place of desperation. We know most times that what we desire won't come true, but it doesn't stop us from having those feelings. There is always the desire to be with the person YOU love, forgetting a not so tiny detail, the person does not love you in the way that will lead to a together forever, down the altar kind of love. I believe that often we push that thought to the deepest recesses of our hearts; at least, I know that is what I did. I could not bear to think I would not have what my heart desired. Psalm 37:4 says, "Delight yourself in the Lord, and He will grant you the desires of your heart" (ESV). Having gone through heartbreak before, I was desperate not to go back there again. Each time you tell yourself, *this* will be the last time, but that is not always the case.

Sadly, I knew from the get-go there was not going to be a future because he never wanted to get married. He wasn't interested in a relationship either. Those were the glaring headlights I should have seen and the honking horn I should have heard. That was a hard truth to accept and live with. We shared a beautiful friendship that got messed up for something that was not meant to be. Life gives us opportunities along the way to reflect on who we are, where we are, and the things that we want. I had concluded that this relationship was different because of the attention, devotion, and support given. I never had that before, and I really wanted it. The question then became, 'was he mine to have?' The response came thundering back with a resounding, "NO!" There are some relationships that are meant to remain in the friend zone, and this was one. Inevitably, letting go was what was best for both of us, and I had to start the process; the idea was painful, but holding on hurt even more.

THE DECISION

1 Corinthians 13:4-5 says, "Love is patient, love is kind...it is not self-seeking" (NIV). This scripture resonated deeply with me. When I thought about the decision that must be made, I shuddered at the prospect of voicing my thoughts. When you truly love

someone and know that you aren't right for each other, you must be willing to give them up. Coming to that conclusion wasn't painless, however, when I made that decision and looked in the rearview mirror, I saw what we saved each other from.

It was hard to "woman-up" and put the thought into action. I prayed and had been praying about it for a long while because I knew it had to be done. But first thing's first: I had to confess my sin, repent, and ask for forgiveness for loving outside of God's will for me. I poured everything out before the Lord, including all my feelings. I let Him know that at the end of the day, I wanted His best for my life despite how I felt and the pain I knew was coming.

In my prayer, I simply asked the Lord to show me what to do and to direct the conversation. Kneeling on the roof of my office building and knowing that the end was near, I reached out to my friends and explained that I needed their help to pray with me through this. As I sat down, I heard in my spirit, "But as it is written, Eye hath not seen, nor ear heard, neither have entered into the heart of man, the things which God hath prepared for them that love Him" (1 Cor. 2:9 KJV). It was as if I was hearing this scripture for the very first time; I was overwhelmed with love.

That night the Lord heard my heart's cry, and the same night He provided the opportunity for the conversation to happen. Believe me when I tell you that I had no doubt that the opening was made for me, and I couldn't look past that no matter how I was feeling. At that moment, the romantic relationship ended, but during that time, we remained friends. Looking back, I was not yet ready to be his friend, and I should have taken time to heal and recover, so that sometime later, we could resume our friendship. When we do not grieve our losses, we cannot heal. While our communication was significantly less, and I mean *significantly*, the truth is I had not fully let him go. I did not realize this until later.

I believed he had entered a new relationship, and the understanding that my heart was still tied to him became very clear. While the frequency of our conversations was reduced, my emotions had not subsided. I tried not to think about him and tried even harder to put him out of my mind, but it didn't work. It was then I had to make the choice to look about me, to put myself first, and if that meant breaking all contact, then that is what needed to be done. I made the painful decision to cut off all communication with him, once and for all. You may not agree with how it was done. In retrospect, it was not the best way for me to handle it, however, at that time, it was the best thing I could do for myself. Sometimes for self-preservation, we rush to do things that we believe will help, albeit temporarily.

I had the urge to do *something*, and even though it wasn't well thought out, at least a decision was made. Running away from my feelings and putting distance between us seemed to be the most natural choice. "Out of sight, out of mind," as the saying goes, though I did accomplish the opposite of what I wanted. It can be true that absence makes the heart grow fonder; this was what happened in my case. So, what I did my best to shy away from was still with me every step of the way, just like my shadow. Running from what was inside me, trying to avoid pain, and refusing to face the giant head on, would come back to haunt me.

I was still in love with my best friend, who had moved on with his life. The story ended there for me as he began a new chapter in his. The journey is not easy. It is a process of trusting God, failing and returning, and even failing again. I continue leaning on God with my accountability partners providing added support. The box is now opened, and the contents of my heart on full display, in the light and glare of the sun, where healing and transformation can now begin. Unless the Lord performs a miracle, it will not be an overnight process. I have learned along this journey of love and loss that there is always a message in a mess. We make mistakes, we move on, and sometimes we repeat our mistakes. Hopefully, we will move forward and learn the lessons that were there for us to grow from.

As you are reading this, you may be going through or have gone through something similar. May I encourage you not to become desperate like I was. Don't allow the desire for a relationship to become the "be-all and end-all." Focus on you. Find and fulfil your purpose. Blossom and bloom right where you are.

Colette M. Lawrence

LESSONS LEARNED

Do not allow desperation to become your driving force. The need to be loved, accepted, and in a relationship cannot and should never supersede God's love for you (or me). A desire that overwhelms can cause you to stay where you should not stay and love where you should not love.

Don't read more into a friendship than what is there. It not only leads to heartache and pain but can lead to irreparably damaged relationships.

As a believer, I know the Bible is clear on being unequally yoked, but I was so caught up in my emotions that I deliberately kept overlooking red flags, in the hope that the Lord would save him for me. Ladies, if he is not for you, he is not *for you*. No matter how we pray for it to be so, it will not change the outcome. Learn from my mistakes. I know the waiting process is hard, but I also know the Lord has good plans for us, to prosper us and not to harm us, plans to give us hope and a future (Jeremiah 29:11 NIV). I hope that in our lives, at least in mine, there will be a husband; however, if there is not, then it is well, and that is God's best for me. It is not easy to understand or digest, but God's word remains true and faithful.

DO NOT WALK OUT OF COVENANT WITH GOD for a relationship, it will not be worth it.

CHAPTER 6

No Condemnation

THE WEIGHT

It is so easy to feel dirty, to feel like God has no further use for you and that He has thrown you away because you messed up and stepped outside His will for your life. The feeling of condemnation is like having an albatross around your neck. Under the weight of it, you're drowning with no way out. Have you ever carried a burden coupled with a sense of despair that maybe your creator has abandoned you? I have. I felt very alone under the weight of my sin and the enemy's taunts. Looking back over my life, I still sometimes cringe with regret when the feeling of condemnation washes over me like waves on a seashore. In those moments, I truly forgot that I was forgiven and that the Lord released me from that albatross, that weight, that burden, and that He still loved me. Do you know guilt and shame of the past have no control over us? Yet, when the enemy slithers in like the snake he is, bringing up the past and reminding us of things long forgiven, we act like it is brand new, forgetting we were released. We forget that we are forgiven.

Have you had a season where you felt a deeper spiritual connection to the Lord, and your relationship seemed strong, almost impenetrable? Then the enemy slithers in. He resurrects old sins, bringing an image to mind, and in a split second, your eyes shift from your heavenly Father, and your communion with your Daddy gets sidelined. We can either unwisely gaze too long at that image, forgetting where we are and whose presence we are in, or we can *boldly* dismiss the enemy by continuing our communion with God through prayer and worship. If I am honest, during those times in the middle of my prayer or worship, I get caught up by giving way to the accusers' carefully timed reminder. My mind then wanders to that once broken place in my life, and regret comes rushing in. The sweet, tender communion with my heavenly Father is broken, and remorse that I helped the enemy's plan succeed comes crashing down. The enemy's plan is to get your focus off the Lord, the lover of your soul, and cause you to doubt His love. He wants the attention that belongs to our Lord and Master, and what better way to do this than to resurrect the past?

Romans 8:1 says, "There is therefore now no condemnation to them who are in Christ Jesus, who walk not after the flesh but after the spirit" (KJV). I haven't always appropriated that scripture to my life because although I know the Lord loves and has forgiven me, sometimes I still try to hide from Him when I look at my choices and the things I have done. When that happens, I am reminded that, "Bringing every thought into captivity to the obedience of (Our Lord Jesus) Christ" (2 Corinthians 10:5b KJV) can be applied here.

MOVING ON

How do *you* currently handle *your* past when God is moving you from one level to another? Do you feel you don't deserve it, and wonder why He still wants to use you? He still wants to use you, because, in His eyes, you have never lost your value. Jeremiah 1:5 says, "Before I formed you in the womb, I knew you" (ESV). He knows every bad choice and wrong decision, yet still chose to love us.

We cannot allow memories of the past to take us down an endless rabbit hole of depression, despondency, and discouragement. We may beat ourselves up over our past, but the reality is your past is a testimony that can reach and help someone else. None of our experiences is wasted with God. You can choose to keep it bottled up, *or* you can decide to share with someone who is where you used to be. Telling yourself you should have known better and not given in to the enemy's lies and tricks is just another way of torturing yourself. 2 Corinthians 2: 11 says, "For we are not ignorant of his (the devil's) devices" (KJV), yet I still get caught in his schemes to ambush me. I need the sweet Holy Spirit to help me not fall prey to his trap because, in my strength alone, I will surely fall.

I am determined not to allow the enemy and the accuser of my soul to rub my past in my face. It is a daily fight, and every day we must combat his efforts, knowing that God is with us and His word will keep us.

THE LOVE OF GOD

Have you recognized that when you are down, he leaves you alone, however, the moment you are in intimate fellowship with the Lord and on a spiritual high, he appears? All of this is for you to feel and walk in condemnation. This is not what the Lord wants for any of us. He doesn't condemn, but "He will convict of sin, righteousness and of judgement" (John 16:8 NKJ). The sad truth is in those moments when many of us fall out of relationship with the Lord. I did that when I allowed the weight of my actions to convince me I couldn't stay in the presence of the Lord. I wondered how he could still love me or have further use for me. I wasn't mature enough to recognize that was exactly what the enemy wanted me to think.

For a period, I lived in condemnation. My life, as you have read, contains a series of mistakes, blunders, and missteps.

I failed the Lord many times and got involved and entangled in relationships and addictions, which made me wonder why I deserved His love. I knew God forgave me because His Word clearly says so, but sadly, I could not accept His forgiveness. For a long time, I didn't understand that receiving God's forgiveness was directly linked to being able to extend forgiveness to myself and others. That was a revelation from the Lord; it was like a veil being lifted. This changed my heart, and with the help of friends, prayer partners, and the Holy Spirit, I slowly started to accept the Lord's forgiveness. It took a while, but I finally got it.

The sins of our past though great, are not greater than the love that the Lord has for you and me. His love is immeasurable. The enemy of our souls knows all this, and that is why he will always try to make us feel condemned, less than, and abandoned. Today, if you are in that place of not receiving the Lord's forgiveness and feeling condemned, I pray the Lord to bring His divine revelation to you. We have a choice to make; will you choose condemnation that hinders you from walking purposefully and victoriously, *or* will you choose to surrender to the Holy Spirit's gentle conviction, which leads to repentance and a purpose filled life? My prayer is that you will yield to the Holy Spirit.

Colette M. Lawrence

Let us look to the Word of God, which is our evidence. It says, "If we confess our sins, He is faithful and just to forgive us our sins and to cleanse us from all unrighteousness" (1 John 1:9 ESV). That means cleansing from all lies, deceit, anger, abortions, addictions, adultery, etc. We don't appropriate the forgiveness of the sin with the sin action. I know personally that we get into trouble when we start to weigh our sins against the love God has for us. My prayer is for you to know that no matter the severity of the sin, it cannot outweigh the love that Christ has for you. That love took Him to the cross for you and me and raised Him from the dead: that is immeasurable love.

No matter what you have done or where you've gone, the Lord's love can reach you. You cannot outrun His love. There is a reason the Lord reminds us that "There is therefore now no condemnation to those who are in Christ Jesus" (Romans 8:1a KJV). He knew the enemy would come against us so that we doubt God's love for us. Today, choose to break free from his lies and boldly declare, "I am *not* condemned!" If your life looks anything like mine, you may think that scripture doesn't apply to you, however, choose to believe the word of the covenant keeping God rather than that of the enemy.

Today, as you are reading this book, may you know that you are seated in heavenly places with Christ Jesus, may you be reminded that He loves you with an everlasting love. May you know unequivocally that absolutely nothing, no sin, no height, no depth can separate you from the love of Christ.

Let us walk with our heads held high, a spring in our steps, our gaze fixed, our hearts steadfast knowing that God's forgiveness is complete. His forgiveness is not progressive, it's instant the moment that you and I repent. He does not forgive and then change His mind. He wants us to know our royal heritage and live it. No condemnation. Blessings.

Colette M. Lawrence

LESSONS LEARNED

See myself as God sees me.

Don't allow guilt and shame to cause me to doubt God's love for me.

I will not be defined by my past but will use it as a stepping-stone to my future.

The Word of God does not condemn but draws me to Him with sweet chords of love.

CHAPTER 7

The Seasons of Our Lives

EBB AND FLOW

Seasons look different for each of us; they are uniquely individual. Sometimes we get caught up in those different seasons and miss the beauty and value of the lessons the Lord is teaching us. We get so wrapped up in mountaintop experiences like breakthroughs and miracles that we can miss the life lessons in them that help us grow. These important lessons will help preserve us in the seasons to come. Oftentimes, we get swept up in the euphoria of reaching the summit that we forget we can't stay there. Let's face it, you may be like me, wanting to stretch out the experience for as long as possible, but the Lord did not design the seasons that way. I believe that we will experience that when we get to heaven, where there will be no crying, no heartache, or pain.

It's good to experience the times where everything seems figured out, where all appears to be well, and there is a respite from life's ordeals. So, what makes this mountain-top experience a lesson in humility? It is the fact that we have no control over its beginning or ending. The Lord begins this journey for us at the appropriate time and ends it at the right time for each of us. When I reflect on the pinnacles of my life, I feel so relaxed and comfortable that I neglect the need to continue deepening and strengthening my relationship with the Lord. Periods of rest can cause us to forget we still need The Life-giver.

Experiences can have highs and lows, and amidst the beauty of life's circumstances, there are also difficult and challenging moments. Times of great triumph are especially beautiful, and rejoicing in them is only natural. However, it is important to use them as an opportunity to draw closer to the One who gives us these victories and the grace to celebrate them. The exhilaration of this experience may give the illusion we're keeping ourselves, but it's not true. The Lord lovingly takes us safely up these mountains and keeps us from slipping and falling. When we get weary, He carries us like the good, good Father He is.

THE QUESTIONS

He is the lover of my soul, the bridge over troubled waters, and always by my side as protector. If He carries me to the mountain top, why do I question the hardships of the valley when He keeps me in both places? The answer is I occasionally forget the reason for the seasons of my life. I also lose track of who I serve and who I am in Him.

How do you feel about loss during the high tides of your life? Do you at times question the Lord or ask if He remembers the hardness of the valley experience? Would you love it if He would allow you a moment to breathe? Maybe that's not you, but it's something I would say. The words may differ, but the feeling is the same.

He knows my thoughts afar off, so my questions are no surprise. Job questioned God during his time of great testing, so when I am going through hardships, pain, loneliness, and brokenness, I question the Lord about it. From time to time, I have forgotten the difficulties I experienced were because of my own choices. When I don't wait for His best, and I make decisions without consulting Him, then it is only fair that I reap what I sow.

Colette M. Lawrence

DRAWN CLOSER TO MY FATHER AND FRIEND

The prior chapters have given you a glimpse into the different seasons of my life. Even when I question the hard seasons, I also use them as an opportunity to run to God and draw closer in His presence.

My life may appear like a roller coaster, with many highs and lows, but I hope you will be able to relate to the places I have been through with your own experiences. The seemingly low places forced me to draw a little closer, deepening and strengthening my walk with the Lord. It also increased my trust and confidence in Him. Those times of difficulty drew me into a relationship of friendship with my Father, yes it did. The scriptures remind us that He is the friend that sticks closer than a brother. So many things have happened in my life that I could only share with Him, and I don't mean the watered-down version either. I do not hide anything from Him; I have learned to bear it all. Even though He already knows it all anyway, He still wants me to take it to Him. It is out of this friendship that I drew close in prayer and intercession. While my love for prayer deepened during this time, it also helped to further shape and form my character. It is a constant reminder to me that I am not alone.

I had experienced this in moments of grief and tragedy when I reached out to Him. Regardless if I was upset or angry, I shared with Him how I was feeling,

POSITIONED *For* PURPOSE

and there was an awareness of His presence that pulled me closer. One of the lessons I learned along the way that I apply to this very day, is that no matter what, I do not run away from His presence. It doesn't matter what season I am going through. The times I stopped communicating and ran away because of hurt, were the moments where I made the worst decisions and suffered the most.

As I learned this lesson and tried my hardest to maintain my relationship with the Lord, I encourage you to do the same. Do not allow the seasons of your life to dictate your relationship with the Lord, instead use them as building blocks to continue building up and shoring up your relationship with Him. We seldom run away from friends and stop communicating with them when difficulties arise. Usually, we go to them seeking comfort, their advice, or just a listening ear. Let's choose to maintain and nurture our relationship, our friendship with the one who is the lover of our souls and the lifter of our heads. It is *He alone* who controls the seasons of our lives.

THANKSGIVING

Let me ask you again, how do you respond to the seasons of your life? Do you see them as preparation for the next level, as preparing you for purpose, or do you see them as moments of rest between your journeys? I find my answers in all three. In the perfect Christian life, my answer would be that I use it to build, but I want to be transparent with myself and you. While building and preparation for what lies ahead in my purpose journey is the ideal, it is not always what I do in the rest period.

Maybe you're asking what rest period I am speaking of. My life seems to be a never-ending train of disappointment, hurt, pain, abandonment, heartaches etc., and if there is or was a moment of rest, I do not see it. I would agree with you (smile) but reflect with me for a minute on your most difficult season. Run the tape in your mind slowly. *Now* can you see what door opening you never expected? Do you remember the peace you felt in that crucial moment of your life? It may appear as just a glimmer, a small dot, however, don't look at the size, just look at the fact that it was there. I know how you feel; how could I have missed that moment during anguish, hurt, and pain when God was there giving me hope and a reason to go on. We miss the move of God when we start classifying things as big or small. When we focus only on what may seem bigger, we miss the good things that God has done.

Set aside time to reflect on your day or reflect on your year, and as Solomon says in Ecclesiastes chapter 3, "To everything there is a season and a time for every matter under heaven" (ESV). Encourage yourself to learn from the seasons.

Ask the Lord to prepare you for the purpose He has in store for you. Thank Him for the lessons that He has taught you. Thank Him for keeping you in times when you wanted to let go, for preserving you when you should have died, for being your anchor and firm foundation. For being your bridge over troubled waters, for being the lifter of your head and the one who held you when you would have given up. Thank Him for the seasons. He allowed them so we could be strengthened for the task He has in store for us. It is preparation for purpose, so prepare yourself.

Colette M. Lawrence

LESSONS LEARNED

In every season, there is a lesson for us to learn. Let's learn it and move on.

Use not only the hard and difficult seasons but the mountaintop experiences as well to draw closer to God.

Give thanks always and allow nothing to hinder our relationship with our heavenly Father.

Set aside time to reflect on our life, at the end of the day, week, month, or year.

CHAPTER 8

Positioned For Purpose

THE WORD

Romans 8:28 says, "And we know that God causes everything to work together for the good of those who love God and are called according to His purpose for them" (NLT). This is a very familiar scripture for me. In my deepest and darkest moments, when it appeared all hope was lost, and I could not see the good in the challenge I was facing, that was the scripture I heard repeatedly. It would always go something like this, "Colette, all things work together for good," and honestly, at that time, I was never in a place to receive that word. I thought it was a cop out for believers when they don't know what to say to encourage the other person. I truly could not see how disappointment, distress, discouragement, despair, and divorce could work out for my good. It would take me years later to appreciate and understand what this scripture represents to a believer facing life's challenges.

The first time I recall hearing this scripture, I was going through a separation that would later lead to divorce. In hindsight, the scripture was not relevant then. Can you imagine going through something so devastating, and instead of hearing that God will deliver, you hear, "all things will work together for your good?" How could I appropriate that with what I was going through? Didn't the Lord see how much I was hurting, that my family was being torn apart? In retrospect, it was the best word for me, however, I was not in a place to accept and receive that word. Only now can I fully understand how it brings comfort and hope. It is a constant reminder that I am loved and that the end will always be better. I know it would not have taken the pain away, but it would have helped me on the path I was on.

THE PATH

My birth family and where I was raised were no accidents. In reflecting on my life's journey, I realize every decision I made, whether good or bad helped me; it just didn't seem that way then. Everything I was going through was positioning me for the purpose and call that God has on my life. The same goes for you, you may not know it yet, or maybe you do.

We tend to either hide or discard the hard parts or seasons of our lives, like when we made bad decisions, wrong choices, or entered wrong relationships. On the other hand, we applaud and glorify the good parts, the successful seasons, where life is sweet. How can we meaningfully connect with others if we aren't willing to share both sides, the good and the bad? Can we really empathize with another person if we aren't open to doing this?

Now that I have matured and understand that this road of life has seasons, I appreciate the fact even more that 'all things' literally means *'ALL THINGS.'* God uses the bumps in the road, the shallow pits, the open graves as well as the smooth paths or stones for his glory. Our journeys look different, and the paths taken were certainly different, yet I believe that it all leads us to find our purpose in Christ. What is the real purpose behind all we have been through and accomplished? Why did God allow these experiences, and what does He want us to learn from them?

POSITIONED

For a long time, I did not think about my life as leading toward a greater purpose than what I saw in the immediate. My job was good, and church was good. I was involved and loved serving others, and still do, yet it felt as though something was missing.

Colette M. Lawrence

The question then became, how can I glorify God through the *'all things'* of my life, and what is the meaning of this deep longing that I had to be and do more? Would I allow Him to use the mess of my life as a message for His glory? Christ is the only one that can satisfy the deep longings of our hearts, but only if we allow Him to.

WALKING IN PURPOSE

Two years ago, I started paying attention to this deep longing and sought to know the reason I was created and how God wanted to use my life for His glory. As His plans unfolded, I heard the Spirit of the Lord say, "It's time to get out of the boat, ankle deep, knee deep." It was scary, and when I turned 50, I left the comfortable for the uncomfortable, the known for the unknown, and decided to take God at His word. If I told you that it was easy to do, I would be lying, but there is a sweet satisfaction in knowing that I am living out what I was created for and called to do. There is no feeling like it. When the days get hard as they sometimes do, and the seasons change as they will, I return to Jeremiah 29:11, "For I know the plans I have for you," says the LORD, "they are plans for good and not for disaster, to give you a future and a hope (NLT).

My prayer for you is that you do not miss out on what our Lord has called you to do. Pay attention to what He is saying to you and move accordingly. He has you, and He will never let you fall. All your mistakes and successes, failures and hardships, heartaches and pain lead to this one thing, *"And we know that all things work together for good to those who love God, to those who are the called according to His purpose"* (Romans 8:28 NKJV).

Colette M. Lawrence

LESSONS LEARNED

> None of our experiences is wasted.

> Know without a shadow of a doubt that God has designed and created us to fulfill His purpose here on earth.

> Our past may look like it cannot be used, but God has a plan for it, and it is good.

> Leave this world empty, using up all that God has placed in us to do.

CONCLUSION

Life has a way of throwing us curveballs, sometimes we miss them, and at other times we don't. Then there are the decisions and wrong choices we make that produce less than desirable outcomes. Sometimes we get lost in the tug of war of daily living that we feel like giving up, but we have a choice of either tugging for our life or giving up. The choice should be easy; tug for your life because everything depends on it.

It is easy to get caught up in what was, what could have been and what should have been and forget that we are in the race of our lives. In this race, we are guaranteed victory, and the caveat is that we must stay in the battle because it is already won. Let us forget the past, live in the present, and look forward to the future. We do not want life to pass us by while our focus and attention are on what we did not achieve, what we didn't get. Instead, let us learn the lessons and move on.

I know you are saying, "Colette, it's not easy to let go." I know, and I understand. It is not easy, however, there is a lot of goodness and grace ahead of us, but if we continue to hold onto the past, there won't be room to break free and embrace the future. As women and as sisters, if we don't let go of the past, we will be stuck, and that is no place for us. It is imperative we break free for emotional, psychological, and mental wellbeing and for others coming behind to know that just as we overcame, so can they.

Our stories of setbacks, trials, triumphs, and overcoming adversity must be shared with at least one person. Someone is waiting on us to stand in the gap for and with them. Someone is waiting on us to tell them that we have been there. We need to let them know it will get better. They need to hear we have been where they are or where they have been. It was rough, difficult, and maybe it was devastating, but if they decide to let go of the hurt, mistakes, regrets, disappointments, and heartbreak of the past, they will soar. They must know all they are going through and will go through; God is working it out for their good. He will use their stories to position and prepare them for the purpose for which they were created.

A sister needs you to remind her that although it seems as if God is not there or is unconcerned, and doesn't care. That's not true, He is right there. He is waiting with outstretched arms to receive her. Reaffirm her that she is not condemned but redeemed. The price paid for our sin and shame is more than the weight and burden of our sins. Christ's love for us is beyond our limited comprehension, and although she may be aware of this love, she may not see herself in that frame, she needs a gentle reminder. Be the woman that lovingly and gently reminds her of God's love, "For God so loved the world that He gave His only begotten Son, that whoever believes in Him should not perish but have everlasting life" (John 3:16 NKJV).

You are reading this book, Positioned for Purpose, and although our stories and paths may be different, I want you to know that you too can break free from the sting of rejection, low self-esteem, lack of self-confidence, depression, and unrequited love. You are not alone, and your past does not define you, Christ does.

He says we are precious in His sight; we are not victims, we are victors. He says He loves us with an everlasting love. He says we are created in His image and likeness. He says we are loved. Let us allow Him to make something beautiful out of the tapestry of our lives and position us for His glory.

MY PRAYER FOR US

Father, thank you for every person who is reading this book right now. I give you thanks for the good plans that you have for their lives.

You see and know what they are going through or will go through, and in knowing that, you still chose to love them in the same that you loved me. I know that their hearts may be hurting or breaking or broken in many pieces, and it seems hard to put the pieces back together, but as the potter, put the pieces back together.

Daddy, I pray that they will allow you to. I know that it is hard because they can't see you and are wondering where you are, but please, may you remind them that you are keeping and preserving them. Lord, you have so much in store for their lives, and I thank you that you are working all things together for our good. So, Father, today I commit us individually and collectively before you, and I ask that you have your way and use us for your glory and honor.

We have a story to tell to the nations, and we thank you that our voices will be heard and your name will be glorified. I give you all the praise, glory, and honor in Jesus's name, Amen!

www.ingramcontent.com/pod-product-compliance
Lightning Source LLC
Chambersburg PA
CBHW051700040426
42446CB00009B/1226